LOOK...AND LOOK AGAIN!™

LOST IN THE HAUNTED MANSION

Story by Maria Tropea

Illustrated by A. Tallarico

Incorporated

Copyright © 1991 Kidsbooks Inc. and
A. Tallarico

All rights reserved including the
right of reproduction in any form.
Manufactured in the United States of America

D1153971

ANSWERS ON LAST PAGE

One day, Melissa and Daniel were outside playing.

"I wonder what's in that old mansion on the hill?" asked Melissa.

"Let's go find out," answered Daniel, "but we'd better be careful not to get lost."

LOOK AND LOOK AGAIN FOR:
Heart · Coffeepot · Football · Hat · Old tire
Dog · Helicopter · Cup · Moon face
Tombstone · Turtle · Monster bird

1313

3

They opened the big wooden door with a CREEAAK! Inside, the furniture was covered with dusty sheets.

"It looks spooky in here," said Daniel. "I think one of those sheets just moved!"

"Don't be silly," said Melissa. "Let's go in and have a look."

LOOK AND LOOK AGAIN FOR:
Six ghosts
Two keys
Jack-o'-lantern
Three skulls
Two mice
Three stars

4

Melissa spotted a staircase.

"Let's see what's upstairs," she whispered.

"After you," said Daniel.

Upstairs, they opened the first door and found a real Sleeping Beasty! As they entered the room, the door closed behind them. Neither Melissa nor Daniel could get it open.

"Oh no!" said Melissa, "Now we're stuck here!"

LOOK AND LOOK AGAIN FOR:
At least ten things that are
wrong with this picture.

Daniel saw another door and said, "Maybe this is a way out." He opened it and SCREEEEEECH!!! It was a closet full of angry bats!

Each bat has an exact twin—except one.

Match the twin bats and LOOK AND LOOK AGAIN FOR the bat without one.

8

Melissa and Daniel ran from the bats. Another door led to a staircase that only went up. They climbed higher and higher until they reached an attic filled with lots of old things. "Melissa," said Daniel, "I think we're lost!"

LOOK AND LOOK AGAIN FOR:
Feather · Paintbrush · Shovel · Yo-Yo · Record
Balloon · Heart · Mouse · Candle · Snake

11

Daniel found a tunnel to crawl through that led them into a kitchen cabinet. Sitting at the table were some GHOSTS having dinner!

"This house is definitely weird!" said Melissa.

LOOK AND LOOK AGAIN FOR:
At least twelve things
that are wrong with this picture.

Quietly, they slipped out of the kitchen and entered a dusty library. There they found lots of scary-looking books.

"I wouldn't want to read these at night," said Melissa.

"Let's go," said Daniel. "It's getting late and we still haven't found a way out of this house."

LOOK AND LOOK AGAIN FOR:
The witches and ghosts
that appear on the books.
How many of each can you find?

15

Daniel accidentally leaned on a bookcase that spun around and pushed them into a secret room. Suddenly, everything was pitch black! All they could see were EYES—that were looking at them! They tried to leave, but now the floor was moving!

LOOK AND LOOK AGAIN FOR:
Five pairs of green eyes
Two pairs of yellow eyes
Eight pairs of red eyes
Four pairs of blue eyes

WHOOSH!!! Melissa and Daniel stepped on
a trap door and slid into another strange room.
At least they were away from those eyes.

LOOK AND LOOK AGAIN FOR:
At least ten things that are wrong with this picture.

19

Then Daniel found some footprints. There were lots of them, but one set led to a window.

"Let's follow them," said Melissa. "Maybe that's the way out!"

LOOK AND LOOK AGAIN FOR:
The one path that leads to the window.

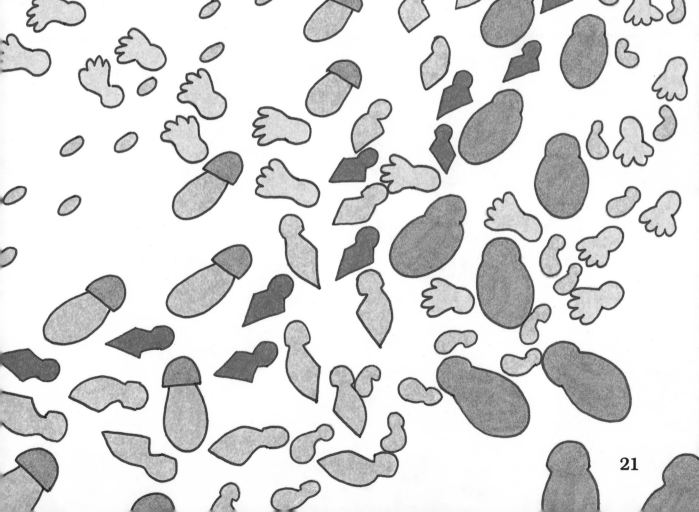

Daniel and Melissa pushed the window up and stepped out into the sunlight. They turned and saw some monsters waving good-bye.

"Maybe we weren't lost in there, after all," said Melissa.

"You're right," said Daniel. "Let's come back tomorrow and explore the rest of the house."

LOOK AND LOOK AGAIN FOR:
Ghost • Kite • Moon • Star
All the letters of the alphabet.

p. 2-3

p. 4-5

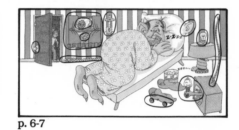
p. 6-7

p. 8-9

p. 10-11

p. 12-13

p. 14-15

8 - RED
5 - GREEN
4 - BLUE
2 - YELLOW

p. 16-17

p. 18-19

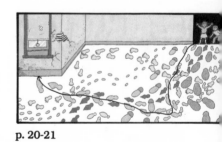
p. 20-21

p. 22-23